Melissa Stewart

ZOOM IN ON LADYBUGS

Enslow Elementary

CONTENTS

WORDS TO KNOW

antennae (an TEN ee)—Two thin body parts on the head of insects and some other animals. Antennae help animals sense the world around them.

larva (LAHR vuh)—The second part in the life cycle of some insects. A larva changes into a pupa.

prey (PRAY)—An animal that is hunted for food.

pupa (PYOO puh)—The third part in the life cycle of some insects. A pupa changes into an adult.

LADYBUG HOMES

ZOOM BUBBLE

Have you ever seen a ladybug? They live in fields and woodlands all over the world.

In places where the winters are cold, they gather in large groups. They rest under rocks or rotting logs.

PARTS OF A LADYBUG

wing

abdomen

leg

eye

antennae

head

thorax

LADYBUG BODY

ZOOM BUBBLE

A ladybug is an insect. An insect has six legs. And its body has three main parts.

An insect's head is in the front. The thorax is in the middle. The abdomen is the part at the back.

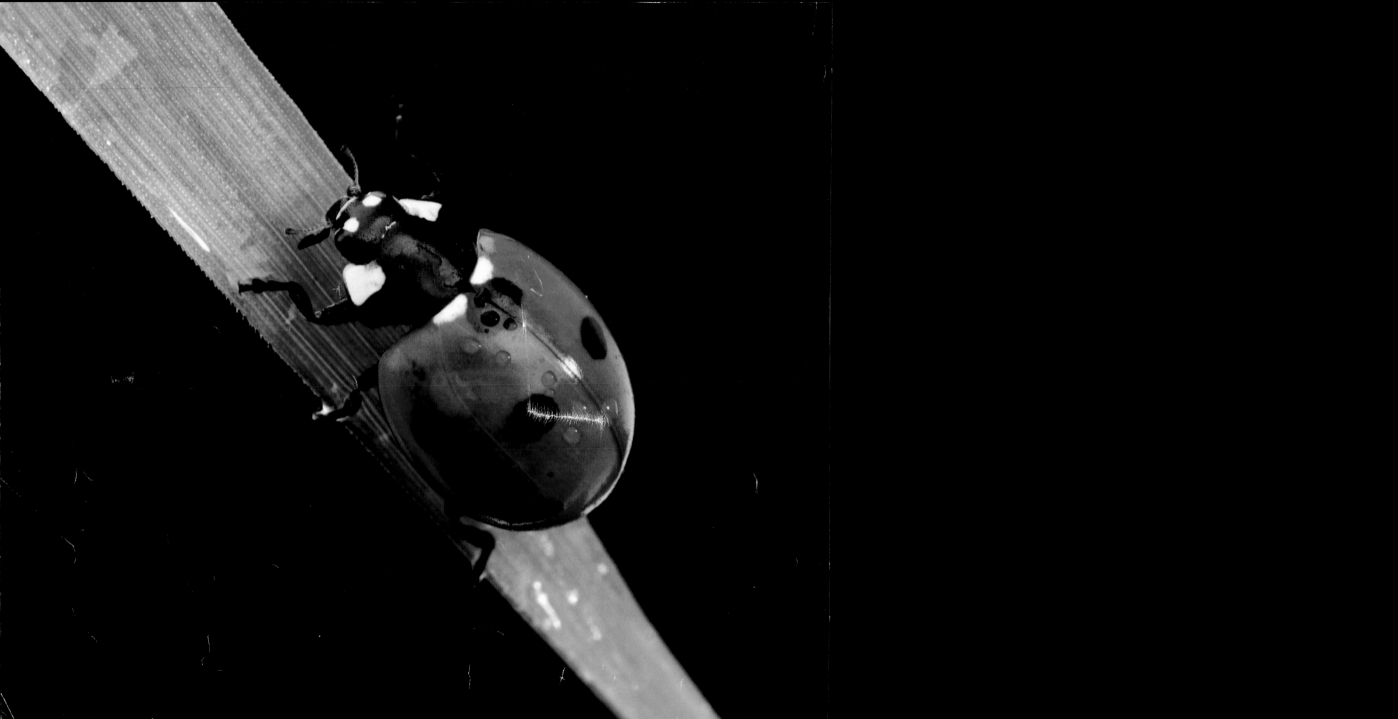

LADYBUG EYES

ZOOM BUBBLE

Can you see this ladybug's eyes? They are black, so they blend in with its head.

The two big eyes don't see very well. They can tell if it is day or night. But they can't see a clear picture of the world.

9

LADYBUG ANTENNAE

ZOOM BUBBLE

A ladybug has two short antennae on its head. They can smell prey. They can also feel and taste.

LADYBUG FOOD

ZOOM BUBBLE

Some ladybugs munch on plants. But most eat small critters. They chow down on small insects, worms, mites, and more.

LADYBUG WINGS

A ladybug has two sets of wings. The hard outer wings protect the soft inner wings.

When a ladybug is ready to fly, it lifts the outer wings. Then it spreads the inner wings and takes off. The inner wings flap through the air.

LADYBUG LEGS

ZOOM BUBBLE

A ladybug has six legs. They are attached to the middle of its body.

When an enemy attacks, a bad-tasting gel oozes out of the ladybug's legs. Yuck! The gross goo makes most attackers spit out their meal.

LADYBUG COLORS

ZOOM BUBBLE

Ladybugs come in different colors. Many have red outer wings with black dots. The head and thorax are black with white spots.

The insect's bright colors send out a message. They say, "Stay away! I taste bad."

LADYBUG LARVAE

ZOOM BUBBLE

Does this ladybug larva look like its parents? No way! First it eats its eggshell. Then it hunts for aphids and other prey.

After about three weeks, the larva looks for a safe place. It sheds its skin and becomes a pupa.

LIFE CYCLE

A ladybug begins life inside an EGG.

A LARVA eats and grows, eats and grows.

ADULT ladybugs can live up to nine months.

The PUPA can't move. But it is going through a lot of changes.

LEARN MORE

BOOKS

Gibbons, Gail. *Ladybugs*. New York: Holiday House, 2013.

Jenkins, Steve. *The Beetle Book*. Boston: Houghton Mifflin Harcourt, 2012.

Posada, Mia. *Ladybugs: Red, Fiery, and Bright*. Minneapolis, Minn.: First Avenue Editions, 2007.

WEB SITES

National Geographic Kids. *Ladybugs.*
<http://kids.nationalgeographic.com/kids/animals/creaturefeature/ladybug>

San Diego Zoo Kids. *Ladybug.*
<http://kids.sandiegozoo.org/animals/insects/ladybug>

INDEX

Enslow Elementary, an imprint of Enslow Publishers, Inc. Enslow Elementary® is a registered trademark of Enslow Publishers, Inc.

Copyright © 2014 by Melissa Stewart

Library of Congress Cataloging-in-Publication Data
Stewart, Melissa.
Zoom in on ladybugs / Melissa Stewart.
p. cm. — (Zoom in on insects)
Summary: "Provides information for readers about a ladybug's home, food, and body"—Provided by publisher.
Includes index.
ISBN 978-0-7660-4215-5
1. Ladybugs—Juvenile literature. I. Title. II. Series: Stewart, Melissa. Zoom in on insects.
QL596.C65S74 2014
595.769—dc23
2012040392

Future editions:
Paperback ISBN: 978-1-4644-0373-6
EPUB ISBN: 978-1-4645-1206-3
Single-User ISBN: 978-1-4646-1206-0
Multi-User ISBN: 978-0-7660-5838-5

Printed in the United States of America
102013 Lake Book Manufacturing, Inc. Melrose Park, IL
10 9 8 7 6 5 4 3 2 1

Series Literacy Consultant:
Allan A. De Fina, PhD
Dean, College of Education
New Jersey City University
Jersey City, New Jersey
Past President of the New Jersey Reading Association

To Our Readers: We have done our best to make sure all Internet Addresses in this book were active and appropriate when we went to press. However, the author and the publisher have no control over and assume no liability for the material available on those Internet sites or on other Web sites they may link to. Any comments or suggestions can be sent by e-mail to comments@enslow.com or to the address on the back cover.

♻ Enslow Publishers, Inc., is committed to printing our books on recycled paper. The paper in every book contains 10% to 30% post-consumer waste (PCW). The cover board on the outside of each book contains 100% PCW. Our goal is to do our part to help young people and the environment too!

Photo Credits: ANATOL ADUTSKEVICH/Photos.com, p. 22 (top left); Christian Skorik/Photos.com, p. 19; Collin Lim/Photos.com, p. 4; et_engineer/Photos.com, p. 11; © iStockphoto.com/David Orr, p. 18; John Foxx/Photos.com, p. 14; Perennou Nuridsany/Science Source, pp. 13, 17; Shutterstock.com, pp. 1, 2, 3, 5, 6, 7, 8, 9, 10, 12, 16, 20, 21, 22 (top right, bottom right, bottom left); Stephen Dalton/Science Source, p. 15.

Cover Photo: Shutterstock.com

Enslow Elementary
an imprint of
Enslow Publishers, Inc.
40 Industrial Road
Box 398
Berkeley Heights, NJ 07922
USA
http://www.enslow.com

Science Consultant:
Helen Hess, PhD
Professor of Biology
College of the Atlantic
Bar Harbor, Maine